BR
WA...S
& AUXILIARIES

TERRY HOLTHAM

HMS Illustrious

THE ROYAL NAVY

Each year we invite a well respected and informed defence journalist to introduce this book as a "guest author" - outlining how they see the current naval scene. This year we welcome Richard Sharpe, Editor of Jane's Fighting Ships to provide our introduction.

"Lack of stress in engineering processes results in products such as gravel". It has taken less than a decade since the end of the Cold War for western military thinking to shift decisively towards an expeditionary strategy as the basis for much of its future equipment procurement priorities. We have been heading in that direction for at least the last five years, but the consensus has been held back by a natural instinct to keep a wary eye on Moscow. It has first been necessary to be as certain as possible that no further seismic changes of direction in the internal affairs of Russia might undermine the feeling of political complacency which grew almost instantly out of the collapse of the Soviet Union. The western military establishment could only resist that complacency for a limited period, although even today Russian technology remains the yardstick against which western naval weapon systems are still developed. Although Russian equipment is still formidable, the current state of naval morale, Fleet maintenance and the shipbuilding industry no longer generates any political stress in western capitals, and only a modicum of concern for the medium term.

Without the identifiable short term military threat of invasion which was the driving force behind defence spending for much of the post second World War period, the western military has been forced to look for an alternative strategy to retain public support. For blue water navies, this has not been hard to define because even during the Cold War much of the live action, as opposed to the preparedness to repel invasion, was found during deployments in support of the so-called 'out of NATO area' activities. These required power projection capabilities, often (but not always) in support of land forces. So the new priorities are merely a case of aligning the policy to fit much of the former actuality, rather than having to seek new employment.

The pendulum of fashionable strategic thinking has now swung so far that we are even talking about building 'land attack destroyers', a concept which is only a whisker away from that of imperialist gunboat, and it is to be hoped that the term will be quietly dropped in favour of something which more accurately reflects the general ubiquity of warships, rather than an implied scenario-dominated specialisation.

Power projection in maritime terms has advantages which cannot be repeated too often. The movement of warships on the high seas requires no prior permission from other governments, and none of the host nation support which is such a severe limitation on the deployment of armies or land-based aircraft. Neither is the assembly of naval and amphibious forces, and their movement towards a potential operating area, an irrevocable escalation of tension, but it can be an unmistakable statement of intent should diplomatic negotiations require the stimulus of the threat of force. Most of the totalitarian regimes which potentially threaten either the lives or the interests of the free world, also live well within reach of the sea.

If maritime strategy has pragmatically shifted its priority towards the coastal region, the most far reaching effects on doctrine are being caused by the explosion in communications capacity. This is not uniformly spread across all the major navies. The US is far ahead of the rest of

2

the field in the development of command systems and, as a result, "interoperability" even with NATO partners is a source of growing concern. Trying to integrate some of the smaller countries into a joint maritime operation can be even more difficult. Sometimes commercial VHF is the only common denominator and even then depends on the quality of an interpreter. This divergence between rich and poor is a key factor when reviewing communications developments. Nonetheless, communications is at the heart of the command revolution which has seen the Joint Force Command Ship or Maritime Battle Centre begin to replace the Flagship in US nomenclature. This has generated the usual battery of "geek-speak" in which terms like Network Centric Warfare are used to describe a concept in which the co-ordination of forces becomes of greater significance than the individual forces themselves. So what's new? The answer is that the battle force commander now has the most interactive communications capacity to exchange data and almost directly control the weapons systems of widely disposed naval and air units, and combine their firepower to achieve instant and massive responses to any designated threat.

One a more trivial level, one US aircraft carrier crew during a six-month deployment in 1997 sent over two million email messages to friends and families, and another carrier recorded that 650 personal computers were carried on board.

This enormous volume of traffic, both professional and personal, is possible because military and civilian satellite capacity and computer software have expanded exponentially in both volume and speed. While many enthuse over the prospects for changing the face of future warfare, some of those at the coalface are keen to point out that this is all happening in a benign satellite electronic environment, and that evolving doctrines must take more account of the effects of future hostile actions against the space-based hardware, the communications links and the controlling computer software.

First of these potential weaknesses is the vulnerability of the satellite uplink to geolocation at UHF and SHF frequencies. Typically, the beamwidth of a 40 cm signal antenna at SHF is about seven degrees, which is easily detected from space or terrestrial platforms some way off, and equally easily degraded either by enemy action or by mutual interference from friendly radars, decoys or own ships' jammers. There are both technical and tactical fixes to alleviate this vulnerability, which anyhow reduces significantly once transmissions move up into the EHF bandwith. EHF is more expensive but is an absolute requirement for the future when covert operations are being conducted from hostile territory. Size of aerial and onboard processing power are important factors in the ability to work through up-link jamming at SHF frequencies, but these are not yet options for the type of unit whose survival may depend on remaining undetected.

Downlink satellite signals are also susceptible to jamming, but the feasibility and extent of this threat is either not fully evaluated, or is not yet in the public domain.

Satellite hardware in geostationary orbit is under all circumstances operating in a naturally unfriendly environment, and must have maintenance-free reliability, which does not of course exist. It is also vulnerable in war to space-based destructive systems, to exo-atmospheric nuclear bursts and to high-powered terrestrial lasers. These are not yet the weapons of minor powers, but if war fighting strategy is to become dependent on space system architectures, they are factors which cannot be ignored by the military planners. Nor is the solution to launch more and more satellites a guaranteed safeguard, although it obviously helps.

Another threat is the penetration of defence computer systems by hackers. This is usually only reported when the perpetrators are brought to trial. Even so, it happens often enough to raise significant questions over the potential for hostile disruption and deception of worldwide command systems. There is also a problem of an expanding civilian market spilling over into the frequency spectrum reserved for the military.

The key question, given today's growing communications capacity is whether it supersedes Clausewitz's dictum that "A great part of the information obtained in war is contradictory, a still greater part is false, and by far the greatest part is uncertain". You have to be pretty optimistic to believe that machine talking to machine at hitherto unknown rates of speed and capacity lead to anything other than a greater measure of uncertainty. On the other hand, co-ordination of weapon systems and speed of response is undergoing a truly great leap forward. Bad news if either you or the machine selects the wrong target.

United Kingdom

If I was given a reward for every media person in the UK whose research into some or other aspect of defence spending started with the implied assumption that the role of the military ended with the defeat of the Soviet Union, I would be a very rich man. In the 1997 general election in this country, a six week high-intensity political campaign virtually ignored defence expenditure as a relevant issue, and defence debates in Parliament are as thinly attended as any. Since 1990, overall defence spending and personnel numbers have each been cut by just less than one third. The current rate of investment stands at 2.7 per cent of GDP, which is the lowest since 1934.

In such a climate it is not surprising that the armed forces are short of people, or that the Treasury does everything it can to postpone spending on equipment replacement projects, some of which are acknowledged as critical to the maintenance of key warfare capabilities.

The 1998 Strategic Defence Review is seeking to strengthen the public perception of the role of the services by reviewing and revising the core national interests, but in truth the outcome is yet another rationalisation of defence cuts by playing to the long term (which can always be reviewed again), by invoking the spirit of more combined service co-operation (which gives an illusion of savings and always at the expense of espirit de corps), and doing little to reinforce capabilities which are urgently needed now. Of these, top of the naval list is the replacement air defence ship, cocooned in a rigid collaborative project with the French and Italians, which is proving to be a strong competitor for the longest, most expensive and least effective international naval project in history. You might think that something would have been learned from the NATO frigate fiasco of the early 1990's, but politically, collaboration is always seen as good news and bureaucrats everywhere enjoy the opportunities for establishing international relationships. The Treasury is happy because the spending of serious money is constantly delayed and the only people who suffer are the industries which need the work and, most important of all, the sailors who have to deploy to dangerous places with obsolete technology. Project Horizon is becoming a scandal, and it is to be hoped that the political courage exists in the UK, which of the three countries involved has by far the largest and most urgent requirement for new air defence ships, to break the shackles and actually place some contracts with the shipyards. This can probably only be done by shifting to the looser collaborative format so successfully used by Germany, Netherlands and Spain.

If that is the bad news, there is much that is good. The restoration of operational links with Pacific Rim navies in 1997 demonstrated that a deployment on that scale involving an aircraft carrier group and nuclear submarines can still be achieved by the UK, but not at the moment by any other navy, except of course the USN. This fits the expeditionary strategy priority, as does the similar gathering of the US/UK Task Groups in the Gulf earlier in 1998.

Eastern Asia and the Gulf remain areas of critical national interest in terms of both security and trade (in the widest sense) and the only realistic form of major national military involvement is by the deployment of naval forces, often in support of the United States. To quote the Secretary of State for Defence, "Strong defence is good foreign policy".

A serious dialogue has now been opened on the type of replacement aircraft carriers needed for the next century, and the project is backed by the Air Force which has seen its land-attack Harrier GR 7 integrated into a carrier air wing. The navalisation of the GR 7 started in 1994, and although there are problems with the aircraft's wing span, which is larger than the naval Harrier, most other technical difficulties have been overcome. The increased fixed-wing component of the carrier air wing has highlighted the deck space limitations of the 'Invincible' class, and although the removal of the Sea Dart SAM system will increase the operating space in the margins, the only real solution is a larger ship capable of operating about 40 STOVL aircraft.

After years of delay, ships are finally being built to replace the LPD's, and a new LPH enters operational service this year. The wheel has gone full circle since 1981 when the incumbent Secretary of State for Defence tried to pay off the amphibious ships and sell a new aircraft carrier as surplus to requirements. There are few better examples of why "short-termism" in military procurement is so damaging. Warships with a life span of up to 30 years should never

4

be designed with specific scenarios in mind, even though defining exact uses is so appealing to the bureaucratic mentality. Utility is a navy's strongest contribution to national defence, and many tasks performed during a ship's life bear little relation to the operational requirement document which originally justified its existence. Even the Strategic Missile Submarine is becoming a more active player in roles other than nuclear deterrence. The USN is using two ex-SSBN's to carry dry deck shelters for underwater swimmers, and Russia has one acting as a mother ship for mini submarines.

Europe

Outside the restaurants of Brussels which serve the expanding and unelected ruling bureaucracy of the European Union (EU) it is very difficult to see anything other than an increasingly divided continent in which the rhetoric of union is divergent from the reality of democratic politics. There are at least six categories of countries. Those that are members of both the EU and NATO, those that are members of one but not the other and wish it to remain that way (e.g. Norway, Sweden and Ireland), those that are members of one but not the other and wish to be included in both (e.g. Turkey), those that have been promised membership of one or the other (e.g. Poland and the Czech Republic),those that wish to join both and are being rebuffed (e.g. Romania and Bulgaria) and those that wish to remain outside both organisations but are obtaining special terms (e.g. Ukraine).

Even amongst the countries that are central to future aspirations of a federal European government, France remains semi-detached from NATO and constantly seeks to undermine US involvement in European security issues. Germany, which has always been the largest net contributor to the European Community finances, is showing increasing concern about substituting the fiscal bedrock of the Deutschmark for a soft EU common currency in which virtually every nation willing to join has fudged the original economic criteria for entry. This economic convergence was due to start in January 1999, and the fiscal looseness of the Mediterranean countries seems likely to dominate. Attempts to force a common European Union foreign policy are again strong on rhetoric, but come apart at the seams every time there is an international crisis, whether in the Balkans or the Gulf, or when the interests of competitive commerce arouse national interests, such as in the lucrative markets of an emerging China.

Add to that the fact that America's military budget is currently running at twice the size of all its European allies combined, and that US investment in communications and information technology is about eight times greater than Europe, and it is not difficult to understand American exasperation at having to subsidise European security interests. Even the signing in January 1998 of a Security Charter to the Baltic States, which implies NATO support while stepping cautiously around Russia's anger, came about because of US rather than European pressure.

In such a climate, investment in navies has little political priority, but commitment to the expeditionary strategy is clearly apparent in amphibious ship programmes, at various states of completion in Germany, France, Netherlands, Spain and Italy.

An interesting development was the deployment in the second half of 1997 of separate German and Italian task groups consisting of a couple of frigates and support ships through the Indian Ocean to east Asia, including visits to India, China, Japan and Indonesia. Because such deployments are essentially in support of national self interest and the pursuit of defence equipment markets, they have no great strategic significance, but this could evolve as experience is regained in the logistics of maritime power projection.

Certainly the French, who already have a low key permanent naval presence in support of their dependent territories in the Indian Ocean and Pacific, should be able to contribute a major task force when the nuclear-powered aircraft carrier CHARLES DE GAULLE finally becomes fully operational at the end of 1999. This ship has taken ten years to build and survived numerous defence budget cuts, but it will provide France with a real expeditionary warfare capability which has not been possible with the elderly and unreliable carriers it replaces.

It is to be hoped, but without much confidence, that some attempt will be made by France to support US global initiatives which benefit the industrialised nations. An aircraft carrier air group which is not prepared to integrate its operations with the USN when deployed to the same area, could cause mutual interference of a particularly lethal kind. The indications are that the French Navy understands this rather better than its government.

In the growth industry of European military groupings, which are mostly political gestures adding nothing new in terms of hardware or of command and control capabilities, the latest is the Spanish-Italian amphibious force. This is a brigade-sized group with equal contributions from both countries, and able to respond to NATO and WEU missions in the Mediterranean. The force headquarters is to shift annually between Cadiz and Brindisi, which indicates the political priority. The absence of the French in this formation is also revealing.

It is of course in the Balkans, the eastern Mediterranean and the Black Sea where any thoughts of expeditionary warfare come a very poor second to local confrontations. The Italian naval and maritime paramilitary forces are in the front line of attempts to curb the flow of illegal immigrants seeking to leave behind the horrors of ethnic warfare in the Balkans for the open frontiers of the European Community. Italy also provides the logistics base for UN peacekeepers trying to hold the line in Bosnia. The Italian Navy has been assisting Albania in the repair and return of the remnants of its navy which fled across the Adriatic in the early part of 1997.

After yet another two serious incidents in October 1997 in which the Greek and Turkish navies each claimed hostile acts by the other, intense efforts by NATO were reported to have led to a reconciliation and a plan to set up regional command headquarters at Larissa in Greece and Izmir in Turkey. Both are to be subordinate to the NATO Southern Command in Naples. By manning them with combined Greek and Turkish staffs, a measure of joint control is hoped to be exercised over military activities in the Aegean.

However, in January 1998 Turkey said it would build new bases in northern Cyprus to counter the construction of a new Greek air base in the south. The news that the US administration was to terminate Foreign Military Sales (FM S) credits to both countries in FY99 was hardly surprising but it does not prevent either country adding to their considerable ex-USN inventory of major warships by outright purchase. The 'Kidd' class destroyers have already been mentioned in this context although Australia is also known to be interested.

If an arc of potential flashpoints is drawn through the Balkans, southern Russia, the Caucasus, the Caspian Sea, the Gulf, the Levant and north Africa, the one country in the middle, both in geographic and geopolitical terms is Turkey. That the European Union continues to exclude this country, which is also a long standing member of NATO, reveals much about the priorities of the EU. Meanwhile a deepening military alliance is growing between Turkey and Israel, with the active encouragement of the USA.

In the Black Sea, Russia has finally handed over the remainder of ships allocated to the Ukraine from the former Soviet Black Sea Fleet. Part of the agreement includes the use of facilities for Russian ships at Sevastopol and other Crimean bases, although Russia intends to build up Novorossiysk as the headquarters for an eastern flotilla. After several years of negotiations and numerous 'agreements' subsequently re-negotiated, it might be thought that this would end the affair of the partition of the Black Sea Fleet, but rumbles over the legitimacy of this latest accord over bases are still coming from Kiev, and Russians are not easily going to renounce their claim to the whole Crimean peninsula. The state of both Fleets is such that Turkey is probably now the predominant naval force in the Black Sea.

In Conclusion

No longer faced by an aggressive and monolithic superpower, the threats facing western nations are no less potent for being asymmetric in character. Those threats which can involve maritime forces include substrategic ballistic weapons with NBC warheads, a range of cruise missiles (some of which can be launched from the shore against ships), a global expansion of diesel submarines, growing stocks of sea mines and computer-based disruption of command and control systems.

If, as seems likely, all the major western navies are reworking their strategies to meet the needs of expeditionary warfare and power projection, the issue of interoperability between nations, which has always been important, is also becoming critical.

If there is one thing that the exponential growth in the computer industry ought to have taught us by now, it is that user friendliness and reliability are not high on the manufacturers' list of priorities, nor is it yet in the commercial interests of those who install the kit.

So if the military want some stability, in order that training and operating coherence can be extracted from the impending chaos of a new data deluge which is no longer restrained by communications capacity, it is going to have to say so with a very loud voice. Up to now, such interoperability as exists between different services and different nations has been achieved by the exercising of common practices through shared communications links. This experience is in danger of being submerged in the stampede for information dominance. Certainly within formal alliances such as NATO, someone needs to be doing some disciplined conducting before the whole orchestra starts playing from different scores. And that is in a benign communications exchange environment, before deliberate system disruption and deception becomes a major issue, or the satellite links come under attack.

The US Navy with its natural instinct for innovation, and its comparatively large equipment budget, is showing few signs in public that it has any reservations about chasing the rainbow of this so-called Revolution in Military Affairs. There is a real danger that like all revolutions the outcome may be rather different than expected, bringing new capabilities but also new constraints, and a great deal of potential confusion.

The question of interoperability also arises in the context of joint service planning and operations. The days when navies, armies and air forces did their own thing have long gone. In fact, historically there has always been an overlap between various elements of each service, both in task, training and execution, but the sometimes mindless civilian mantra that decrees that all things collaborative between nations is a good thing, is increasingly spilling over into a similar drive to blur the distinctions between services.

In an academic sense it might not appear to matter whether a helicopter in support of an infantry regiment is flown by a soldier or an airman. Similarly an STOVL aircraft operating from a seaborne platform seemingly might just as well be flown by a sailor, a marine or an airman. In practice it matters very much indeed. This is not because of outdated attachments to historical tribal instincts, but because the ethos and modus operandi of each service has evolved to fit the whole environment in which they are required to perform. Furthermore, each individual service tends to attract and mould the type of personality best suited to its style of work. As an example from the civilian world, London taxi cab and long distance lorry drivers are not interchangeable, although both are employed in driving vehicles on roads.

In parallel with the divisive issue of women at sea, it is now becoming more than a senior officer's career is worth to point out that there are very real distinctions between how each service selects and employs its people, and maintains its equipment, and that these distinctions cannot be discarded without an unquantifiable but potentially serious loss of fighting efficiency. And even those courageous enough to take on these issues in an official sense are likely to be discounted as being unable 'to overcome cultural and institutional inertia and resistance to change'. The environments of the land, the sea and the sky may overlap, but each shows no sign of being about to change its geophysical makeup to fit in with the contemporary fashions of new age politico/military doctrines.

Richard Sharpe

December 1998

SHIPS OF THE ROYAL NAVY
Pennant Numbers

Ship	Pennant Number	Ship	Pennant Number
		BRAVE	F94
Aircraft Carriers			
		LONDON	F95
INVINCIBLE	R05	SHEFFIELD	F96
ILLUSTRIOUS	R06		
ARK ROYAL ●	R07		
		COVENTRY	F98
Destroyers		CORNWALL	F99
		LANCASTER	F229
BIRMINGHAM	D86	NORFOLK	F230
NEWCASTLE	D87	ARGYLL	F231
GLASGOW	D88	MARLBOROUGH	F233
EXETER	D89	IRON DUKE	F234
SOUTHAMPTON	D90	MONMOUTH	F235
NOTTINGHAM	D91	MONTROSE	F236
LIVERPOOL	D92	WESTMINSTER	F237
MANCHESTER	D95	NORTHUMBERLAND	F238
GLOUCESTER	D96	RICHMOND	F239
EDINBURGH	D97		
YORK	D98	**Submarines**	
CARDIFF	D108		
		VANGUARD	S28
Frigates		VICTORIOUS	S29
		VIGILANT	S30
KENT	F78	UPHOLDER ●	S40
PORTLAND	F79	UNSEEN ●	S41
GRAFTON	F80	URSULA ●	S42
SUTHERLAND	F81	UNICORN ●	S43
SOMERSET	F82	TRENCHANT	S91
ST ALBANS	F83	TALENT	S92
CUMBERLAND	F85	TRIUMPH	S93
CAMPBELTOWN	F86	SCEPTRE	S104
CHATHAM	F87	SPARTAN	S105
BOXER	F92	SPLENDID	S106
BEAVER	F93	TRAFALGAR	S107

Ship	Pennant Number	Ship	Pennant Number
TURBULENT	S110	**Patrol Craft**	
TIRELESS	S117		
TORBAY	S118	LEEDS CASTLE	P258
		ARCHER	P264
Assault Ships		DUMBARTON CASTLE	P265
		BITER	P270
FEARLESS	L10	SMITER	P272
INTREPID ●	L11	PURSUER	P273
OCEAN	L12	TRACKER	P274
		RAIDER	P275
Minehunters		ANGLESEY	P277
		ALDERNEY	P278
BRECON	M29	BLAZER	P279
LEDBURY	M30	DASHER	P280
CATTISTOCK	M31	PUNCHER	P291
COTTESMORE	M32	CHARGER	P292
BROCKLESBY	M33	RANGER	P293
MIDDLETON	M34	TRUMPETER	P294
DULVERTON	M35	GUERNSEY	P297
BICESTER	M36	SHETLAND	P298
CHIDDINGFOLD	M37	ORKNEY	P299
ATHERSTONE	M38	LINDISFARNE	P300
HURWORTH	M39		
BERKELEY	M40	**Survey Ships & RN Manned Auxiliaries**	
QUORN	M41		
SANDOWN	M101	GLEANER	A86
INVERNESS	M102	ROEBUCK	H130
CROMER	M103	SCOTT	H131
WALNEY	M104	HERALD	H138
BRIDPORT	M105	EXPRESS	A163
PENZANCE	M106	EXPLORER	A164
PEMBROKE	M107	EXAMPLE	A165
GRIMSBY	M108	EXPLOIT	A167
ORWELL	M2011	ENDURANCE	A171
		IRONBRIDGE	A311
		BULLDOG	H317
		IXWORTH	A318
		BEAGLE	H319

● *Ships in reserve/long refit*

● OFFICIAL PHOTO

HMS Victorious

VANGUARD CLASS

Ship	Pennant Number	Completion Date	Builder
VANGUARD	S28	1992	VSEL
VICTORIOUS	S29	1994	VSEL
VIGILANT	S30	1997	VSEL
VENGEANCE	S31	1999	VSEL

Displacement 15,000 tons (dived) **Dimensions** 150m x 13m x 12m **Speed** 25 + dived **Armament** 16 - Trident 2 (D5) missiles, 4 Torpedo Tubes **Complement** 135

Notes
After the first UK successful D5 strategic missile firing in May '94 the first operational patrol was carried out in early '95 and a patrol has been constantly maintained ever since. Two submarines have two crews each, the other two an extended single "Gold" crew. Construction costs of the last, VENGEANCE, are estimated at £863 million.

● OFFICIAL PHOTO

HMS Superb

SWIFTSURE CLASS

Ship	Pennant Number	Completion Date	Builder
SCEPTRE	S104	1978	Vickers
SPARTAN	S105	1979	Vickers
SPLENDID	S106	1980	Vickers
SOVEREIGN	S108	1974	Vickers
SUPERB	S109	1976	Vickers

Displacement 4,500 tons dived **Dimensions** 83m x 10m x 8m **Speed** 30 knots + dived **Armament** 5 Torpedo Tubes **Complement** 116.

Notes
All are based at Faslane. The class will be replaced in due course by the Batch 2 Trafalgar class boats. (See next page) SPLENDID successfully fired the first Tomahawk missile whilst submerged in November 1998.

11

● OFFICIAL PHOTO

HMS Turbulent

TRAFALGAR CLASS

Ship	Pennant Number	Completion Date	Builder
TRENCHANT	S91	1989	Vickers
TALENT	S92	1990	Vickers
TRIUMPH	S93	1991	Vickers
TRAFALGAR	S107	1983	Vickers
TURBULENT	S110	1984	Vickers
TIRELESS	S117	1985	Vickers
TORBAY	S118	1986	Vickers

Displacement 4,500 tons **Dimensions** 85m x 10m x 8m **Speed** 30 + dived **Armament** 5 Torpedo Tubes **Complement** 125.

Notes

Enhanced development of the Swiftsure Class. Quieter, faster and with greater endurance than their predecessors. It is expected Tomahawk Cruise Missiles will eventually be fitted in all of these boats. Three new Batch II Trafalgar Class vessels (to be named ASTUTE, ARTFUL and AMBUSH) were ordered in 1997.

● MARITIME PHOTOGRAPHIC

HMS Unseen

UPHOLDER CLASS

Ship	Pennant Number	Completion Date	Builder
UPHOLDER	S40	1989	Vickers
UNSEEN	S41	1991	Cammell Laird
URSULA	S42	1992	Cammell Laird
UNICORN	S43	1993	Cammell Laird

Displacement 2,400 tons (dived) **Dimensions** 70m x 8m x 5m **Speed** 20 knots dived **Armament** 6 Torpedo Tubes: Sub Harpoon missile **Complement** 44.

Notes
A new class of conventionally powered submarines. As a result of Defence economies announced in 1993 all the class were paid off during 1994 but remain laid up at Barrow-in-Furness in late 1998. They have been leased to Canada who will take delivery as from 2000

● OFFICIAL PHOTO

HMS Invincible

INVINCIBLE CLASS

Ship	Pennant Number	Completion Date	Builder
INVINCIBLE	R05	1979	Vickers
ILLUSTRIOUS	R06	1982	Swan Hunter
ARK ROYAL	R07	1985	Swan Hunter

Displacement 19,500 tons **Dimensions** 206m x 32m x 6.5m **Speed** 28 knots **Armament** Sea Dart Missile, 2 - 20mm guns, 3 Phalanx/Goalkeeper **Aircraft** 8 - Sea Harrier, 12 - Sea King **Complement** 900 + aircrews.

Notes

Manpower problems have dictated that only two ships are kept in the operational fleet, with the third in refit or reserve. ARK ROYAL is in reserve at Portsmouth but is now due to be refitted at Rosyth in June 1999. The Sea Dart system was removed from ILLUSTRIOUS in 1998 to increase deck space for more aircraft.

● WALTER SARTORI

HMS Ocean

OCEAN

Ship	Pennant Number	Completion Date	Builder
OCEAN	L12	1998	Kvaerner

Displacement 20,000 tons **L.O.A.** 203m **Speed** 19 knots **Complement** Ship 258, Squadrons 180, Embarked force 800.

Notes
The new helicopter carrier was launched in October 1995 at Kvaerner's yard in Glasgow. Sailed November 1996 for fitting out at Barrow during 1997. Was undergoing hot and cold weather trials in late 1998 and expected to enter operational service in mid 1999.

● TERRY HOLTHAM

HMS Fearless

FEARLESS CLASS

Ship	Pennant Number	Completion Date	Builder
FEARLESS	L10	1965	Harland & Wolff
INTREPID	L11	1967	J. Brown

Displacement 12,500 tons, 19,500 tons (flooded) **Dimensions** 158m x 24m x 8m
Speed 20 knots **Armament** 2 - Vulcan Phalanx (FEARLESS only) 2 - 40mm guns, 4 -
30mm **Complement** 580.

Notes
Multi-purpose ships that can operate helicopters for embarked Royal Marine
Commandos. 4 landing craft are carried on an internal deck and are flooded out when
the ship docks down. INTREPID paid off at Portsmouth in 1991 when a decision was
made that both vessels would be replaced. It was reported to Parliament in 1996 that
£32 million had been spent on INTREPID's maintenance since she paid off. That figure
continues to rise. Financial restraints delayed any order being made until 1996 when it
was announced that two new vessels were to be ordered and named ALBION and BUL-
WARK. (The first steel was cut in November 1997). FEARLESS is to be kept operational
until 2002 when the second vessel is expected to be delivered.

16

● MARITIME PHOTOGRAPHIC

HMS Birmingham

SHEFFIELD CLASS
(Type 42) Batch 1 & 2

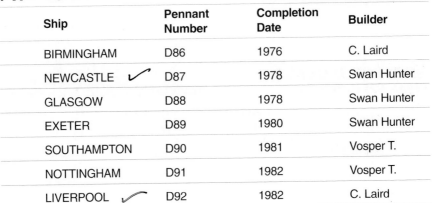

Ship	Pennant Number	Completion Date	Builder
BIRMINGHAM	D86	1976	C. Laird
NEWCASTLE	D87	1978	Swan Hunter
GLASGOW	D88	1978	Swan Hunter
EXETER	D89	1980	Swan Hunter
SOUTHAMPTON	D90	1981	Vosper T.
NOTTINGHAM	D91	1982	Vosper T.
LIVERPOOL	D92	1982	C. Laird
CARDIFF	D108	1979	Vickers

Displacement 3,660 tons **Dimensions** 125m x 15m x 7m **Speed** 29 knots **Armament** 1 - 4.5" gun, 4 - 20mm guns, Sea Dart Missile System: 2 - Phalanx, Lynx Helicopter, 6 Torpedo Tubes **Complement** 280 +.

Notes
Sister Ships SHEFFIELD and COVENTRY lost in 1982 during the Falklands conflict. The first of class for disposal was expected to be BIRMINGHAM in 1999 but continuing delays to the Horizon frigate project could see this postponed.

HMS Edinburgh

SHEFFIELD CLASS
(Type 42) Batch 3

Ship	Pennant Number	Completion Date	Builder
MANCHESTER	D95	1983	Vickers
GLOUCESTER	D96	1984	Vosper T.
EDINBURGH	D97	1985	C. Laird
YORK	D98	1984	Swan Hunter

Displacement 4,775 tons **Dimensions** 132m x 15m x 7m **Speed** 30 knots + **Armament** 1- 4.5" gun, 1- Phalanx, 4 - 20mm guns. Sea Dart missile system. Lynx Helicopter, 6 Torpedo Tubes **Complement** 301.

Notes
"Stretched' versions of earlier ships of this class. Designed to provide area defence of a task force. Deck edge stiffening fitted to counter increased hull stress. Plans continue (with France and Italy) on the requirement for a Common New Generation Frigate to enter service in 2004 but this date seems unlikely to be met.

18

● MARITIME PHOTOGRAPHIC

HMS London

BROADSWORD CLASS
(Type 22) Batch 2

Ship	Pennant Number	Completion Date	Builder
BOXER	F92	1983	Yarrow
BEAVER	F93	1984	Yarrow
BRAVE•	F94	1985	Yarrow
LONDON •	F95	1986	Yarrow
SHEFFIELD •	F96	1987	Swan Hunter
COVENTRY •	F98	1988	Swan Hunter

Displacement 4,100 tons **Dimensions** 143m x 15m x 6m **Speed** 30 knots **Armament** 4 Exocet Missiles, 2 Sea Wolf Missile Systems, 4 - 30mm + 2 - 20mm guns, 6 Torpedo Tubes, 2 Lynx Helicopters **Complement** 273.

Notes
• Ships have enlarged hangar and flight deck. A Sea King can be, and is, carried in some ships of this class. All Batch 1 ships were sold to Brazil 1995-1997. The 1998 Strategic Defence Review resulted in the following reductions to this class being made over the next few years. BOXER, BEAVER and LONDON will be offered for sale in 1999, BRAVE in 2000 and COVENTRY in 2001.

● D CULLEN   **HMS Campbeltown**

BROADSWORD CLASS
(Type 22) Batch 3

Ship	Pennant Number	Completion Date	Builder
CUMBERLAND ✓	F85	1988	Yarrow
CAMPBELTOWN ✓	F86	1988	C. Laird
CHATHAM	F87	1989	Swan Hunter
CORNWALL	F99	1987	Yarrow

Displacement 4,200 tons **Dimensions** 147m x 15m x 7m **Speed** 30 knots **Armament** 1 - 4.5" gun, 1 - Goalkeeper, 8 - Harpoon, 2 - Seawolf, 4 - 30mm guns, 6 Torpedo Tubes, 2 Lynx or 1 Sea King Helicopter **Complement** 250.

Notes
General purpose gun and Goalkeeper system added to these ships as a direct result of lessons learned during Falklands conflict. All these ships have a major anti-submarine capability. Cost £180 million each.

OFFICIAL PHOTO

HMS Cumberland

F214 GERMAN  BLACK
RED
YELLOW

DUKE CLASS (Type 23)

Ship	Pennant Number	Completion Date	Builder
KENT	F78		Yarrow
PORTLAND	F79	1999	Yarrow
GRAFTON	F80	1996	Yarrow
SUTHERLAND	F81	1997	Yarrow
SOMERSET	F82	1996	Yarrow
ST ALBANS	F83		Yarrow
LANCASTER	F229	1991	Yarrow
NORFOLK	F230	1989	Yarrow
ARGYLL	F231	1991	Yarrow
MARLBOROUGH	F233	1991	Swan Hunter
IRON DUKE	F234	1992	Yarrow
MONMOUTH	F235	1993	Yarrow
MONTROSE	F236	1993	Yarrow
WESTMINSTER	F237	1993	Swan Hunter
NORTHUMBERLAND	F238	1994	Swan Hunter
RICHMOND	F239	1994	Swan Hunter

Displacement 3,500 tons **Dimensions** 133m x 15m x 5m **Speed** 28 knots **Armament** Harpoon & Seawolf missile systems: 1 - 4.5" gun, 2 - single 30mm guns, 4 - 2 twin, magazine launched, Torpedo Tubes, Helicopter **Complement** 157.

Notes
An order was placed in 1996 for three more vessels to be named PORTLAND(1999) KENT (2000) and ST ALBANS (2001). Delivery dates in brackets. No further orders are now likely to be placed

HMS Northumberland

● OFFICIAL PHOTO

HMShips Hurworth &Atherstone

MINE COUNTERMEASURES SHIPS (MCMV'S) HUNT CLASS

Ship	Pennant Number	Completion Date	Builder
BRECON	M29	1980	Vosper T.
LEDBURY	M30	1981	Vosper T.
CATTISTOCK	M31	1982	Vosper T.
COTTESMORE	M32	1983	Yarrow
BROCKLESBY	M33	1983	Vosper T.
MIDDLETON	M34	1984	Yarrow
DULVERTON	M35	1983	Vosper T.
BICESTER	M36	1986	Vosper T.
CHIDDINGFOLD	M37	1984	Vosper T.
ATHERSTONE	M38	1987	Vosper T.
HURWORTH	M39	1985	Vosper T.
BERKELEY	M40	1988	Vosper T.
QUORN	M41	1989	Vosper T.

Displacement 625 tonnes **Dimensions** 60m x 10m x 2.2m **Speed** 17 knots **Armament** 1 x 30mm + 2 x 20mm guns **Complement** 45.

Notes

The largest warships ever built of glass reinforced plastic. Their cost (£35m each) has dictated the size of the class. Very sophisticated ships – and lively seaboats! All based at Portsmouth and Faslane. Ships are frequently deployed in the Fishery Protection role During 1998 COTTESMORE, BRECON and DULVERTON replaced the River Class vessels in the Northern Ireland squadron.

● CHRIS ROGERS

HMS Orwell

FLEET MINESWEEPERS
RIVER CLASS

Ship	Pennant Number	Completion Date	Builder
ORWELL	M2011	1985	Richards

Displacement 850 tonnes **Dimensions** 47m x 10m x 3m **Speed** 14 knots **Armament** Nil **Complement** 30.

Notes
Sole survivor of a class of MCM ships built for service with the RNR. All were withdrawn during 1994 as a result of the 1993 defence economies. ORWELL is a training ship (for navigational and initial sea experience) attached to BRNC Dartmouth. BLACKWATER, ITCHEN, SPEY and ARUN sold to Brazil in 1998.

HMS Cromer

SANDOWN CLASS

Ship	Pennant Number	Completion Date	Builder
SANDOWN	M101	1989	Vosper T.
INVERNESS	M102	1991	Vosper T.
CROMER	M103	1991	Vosper T.
WALNEY	M104	1992	Vosper T.
BRIDPORT	M105	1993	Vosper T.
PENZANCE	M106	1998	Vosper T.
PEMBROKE	M107	1998	Vosper T.
GRIMSBY	M108	1999	Vosper T.

Displacement 450 tons **Dimensions** 53m x 10m x 2m **Speed** 13 knots **Armament** 1 - 30mm gun **Complement** 34.

Notes
A class dedicated to a single mine hunting role. Propulsion is by vectored thrust and bow thrusters. Up to 15 more ships were planned, but the 7 due to be ordered in 1991 were postponed until 1994. The last to be delivered will be (acceptance dates in brackets) BANGOR (00), RAMSEY (00), BLYTH (01), SHOREHAM (01). CROMER is due for early disposal in 1999 in lieu of refit.

26

● MARITIME PHOTOGRAPHIC

HMS Dumbarton Castle

CASTLE CLASS

Ship	Pennant Number	Completion Date	Builder
LEEDS CASTLE	P258	1981	Hall Russell
DUMBARTON CASTLE	P265	1982	Hall Russell

Displacement 1,450 tons **Dimensions** 81m x 11m x 3m **Speed** 20 knots **Armament** 1 - 30mm gun **Complement** 40

Notes
These ships have a dual role – that of fishery protection and offshore patrols within the limits of UK territorial waters. Unlike the Island Class these ships are able to operate helicopters – including Sea King aircraft. DUMBARTON CASTLE is on long term deployment to the Falkland Islands with her ships' company rotating every four months.

● MARITIME PHOTOGRAPHIC

HMS Orkney

ISLAND CLASS

Ship	Pennant Number	Completion Date	Builder
ANGLESEY	P277	1979	Hall Russell
ALDERNEY	P278	1979	Hall Russell
GUERNSEY	P297	1977	Hall Russell
SHETLAND	P298	1977	Hall Russell
ORKNEY	P299	1977	Hall Russell
LINDISFARNE	P300	1978	Hall Russell

Displacement 1,250 tons **Dimensions** 60m x 11m x 4m **Speed** 17 knots **Armament** 1 - 30mm gun **Complement** 39.

Notes
Built on trawler lines these ships were introduced to protect the extensive British interests in North Sea oil/gas installations and to patrol the 200 mile fishery limit. All vessels have extra crew members to allow leave to be taken and thus extend vessels time on task over the year. ORKNEY will be paid off in April 1999 as a result of the 1998 Strategic Defence Review. and reduced commitments in Scottish waters.

● MARITIME PHOTOGRAPHIC

HMS Raider

COASTAL TRAINING CRAFT
ARCHER CLASS

Ship	Pennant Number	Completion Date	Builder
ARCHER	P264	1985	Watercraft
BITER	P270	1985	Watercraft
SMITER	P272	1986	Watercraft
PURSUER	P273	1988	Vosper
TRACKER	P274	1998	Ailsa Troon
RAIDER	P275	1998	Ailsa Troon
BLAZER	P279	1988	Vosper
DASHER	P280	1988	Vosper
PUNCHER	P291	1988	Vosper
CHARGER	P292	1988	Vosper
RANGER	P293	1988	Vosper
TRUMPETER	P294	1988	Vosper

Displacement 43 tonnes **Dimensions** 20m x 6m x 1m **Speed** 20 knots **Armament** Nil
Complement 14.

Notes
In service with RN University units. TRUMPETER and RANGER deployed to Gibraltar
in 1991.

● OFFICIAL PHOTO **HMS Scott**

SCOTT CLASS

Ship	Pennant Number	Completion Date	Builder
SCOTT	H 131	1997	Appledore

Displacement 13,300 tonnes **Dimensions** 130m x 21.5m x 14m **Speed** 17 knots **Complement** 63

Notes

Ordered in January 1995 from BAeSEMA - the first prime contract for a new ship to be placed by MoD with a firm other than a shipbuilder. Handed over in June 1997 after trials. SCOTT carries a mixture of the latest UK and US survey equipment. The sonar system is US supplied. The ship is fully RN "lean manned" with a complement of 63 which operates in a 3 watch crew rotation system; 42 personnel are embarked at any one time. It is expected she will be at sea for some 300 days per year. These man-power reductions over previous survey ships have been possible because of the extensive use of commercial lean manning methods including unmanned machinery spaces, fixed fire fighting systems and extensive machinery and safety surveillance technology. Based in the Far East throughout 1999.

All Survey Ships had their pennant numbers changed from the "A" prefix to "H" prefix in 1998.

● MARITIME PHOTOGRAPHIC

HMS Roebuck

ROEBUCK CLASS

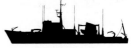

Ship	Pennant Number	Completion Date	Builder
ROEBUCK	H130	1986	Brooke Marine

Displacement 1500 tonnes **Dimensions** 64m x 13m x 4m **Speed** 15 knots **Complement** 47.

Notes
Survey ship able to operate for long periods away from shore support, this ship and the other vessels of the Hydrographic Fleet collect the data that is required to produce the Admiralty Charts and publications which are sold to mariners worldwide. Fitted with the latest fixing aids and sector scanning sonar. An order for new vessels to replace ROEBUCK and BEAGLE/BULLDOG was expected during 1996 but the tendering exercise (only) is now delayed until 1999.

HMS Herald

HECLA CLASS

Ship	Pennant Number	Completion Date	Builder
HERALD	H138	1974	Robb Caledon

Displacement 2,733 tons **Dimensions** 79m x 15m x 5m **Speed** 14 knots **Complement** 115.

Notes
An order for a new vessel to replace HERALD is now expected during 1999.

● D HANNAFORD

HMS Bulldog

BULLDOG CLASS

Ship	Pennant Number	Completion Date	Builder
BULLDOG	H317	1968	Brooke Marine
BEAGLE	H319	1968	Brooke Marine

Displacement 1,088 tons **Dimensions** 60m x 11m x 4m **Speed** 15 knots
Complement 39.

Notes
Designed to operate in coastal waters. Both have been extensively refitted to extend hull life. An order for new vessels to replace both ships was expected during 1998. GLEANER (A86) is a small inshore survey craft based at Portsmouth.

● D HANNAFORD

HMS Endurance

ICE PATROL SHIP

Ship	Pennant Number	Completion Date	Builder
ENDURANCE	A171	1990	Ulstein-Hatlo

Displacement 5,129 tons **Dimensions** 91m x 17.9m x 6.5m **Speed** 14.9 knots **Armament** Small arms **Aircraft** 2 Lynx **Complement** 113.

Notes
Chartered for only 7 months in late 1991 to replace the older vessel of the same name. Originally M/V POLAR CIRCLE, renamed HMS POLAR CIRCLE (A176) and then purchased by MOD(N) and renamed again in October 1992 to current name.

34

● MARITIME PHOTOGRAPHIC   Explorer

COASTAL TRAINING CRAFT
ARCHER CLASS

Ship	Pennant Number	Completion Date	Builder
EXPRESS	A163	1988	Vosper T
EXPLORER	A164	1985	Watercraft
EXAMPLE	A165	1985	Watercraft
EXPLOIT	A167	1988	Vosper T

Displacement 43 tons **Dimensions** 20m x 6m x 1m **Speed** 20 knots **Armament** Nil
Complement 14

Notes
Former Example Class Training vessels for the RNXS - until the organisation was disbanded on 31 March 1994. Vessels were then transferred to RN University Units as sea training tenders. (See also page 29)

● C. HOCKADAY

Colonel Templer

Ship	Pennant Number	Completion Date	Builder
COLONEL TEMPLER		1966	Hall Russell

Displacement 1,300 tons **Dimensions** 56m x 11m x 5.6 m **Speed** 12 knots
Complement 14

Notes

Built as a stern trawler but converted in 1980 for use by the Defence Research Agency as an acoustic research vessel. A major rebuild was completed after a serious fire gutted the ship in 1990. 12 scientists can be carried. Operated by contractors.

> *A number of merchant ships are on charter to various MOD departments. They include MAERSK GANNET, MAERSK ASCENCION, ST BRANDAN, INDOMITABLE and OIL MARINER in support of the Falkland Island commitment. PROUD SEAHORSE and MARINE EXPLORER have hydrographic roles in UK waters.*

SHIPS ORDERED FOR THE FUTURE FLEET...

GEC-MARINE (BARROW) FORMERLY VSEL

ASTUTE/AMBUSH/ARTFUL - The 1st of the Class were ordered in March 1997 to replace the oldest units of the S class. Work is due to commence on ASTUTE in 1999. The other 2 will follow at yearly intervals. Nevertheless, it will not be until 2005 that ASTUTE will commission (3.5 years later than originally intended), replacing SPARTAN which decommissions the following year. AMBUSH will replace SUPERB in 2007 and ARTFUL replaces SCEPTRE in 2008. Costs are estimated at £650m per boat.
The 1998 Strategic Defence Review (SDR) has confirmed that 2 more vessels will be ordered in due course. They will replace the first and second of the Trafalgar Class.
WAVE KNIGHT/WAVE RULER - Two Auxiliary Oilers were ordered in March 1997 as replacements for the ageing fleet tankers OLWEN and OLNA. Construction has already commenced. (Further orders are likely to replace the 3 ship Rover Class in due course).
ALBION/BULWARK - After some considerable delay the replacements for FEARLESS and INTREPID were ordered in July 1996. Acceptance is scheduled for March 2002 and 2003, delays of 41 and 27 months respectively on the original in service dates. ALBION will cost about £340m and BULWARK some £255m.

GEC-MARINE (YARROW)

KENT/ST ALBANS/PORTLAND - The last of the Duke Class Type 23 frigates were ordered in February 1996. KENT was launched in May 1998 and work commenced on ST ALBANS in December 1997. Costs are £170m apiece.

VOSPER THORNYCROFT (V.T.)

BANGOR/RAMSEY/BLYTH/SHOREHAM - Work commenced on BANGOR in March 1998. The present orders were placed in July 1994 and will have been completed by 2001. Cost is about £35m apiece.
R.V. (Research Vessel) TRITON - In July 1998, the Defence Evaluation and Research Agency placed a £13m order with V.T. for the construction of a 2/3 scale research warship to evaluate a trimaran hull form as a replacement for the Type 23 frigate. TRITON will be 90m long with a displacement of 1100 tons. She will have all-electric propulsion. Construction will commence in 1999 - sea trials can be expected early in 2001.

FUTURE ORDERS

There is the likelihood of a number of orders in 1999 (maximum of 9)

LSL (Landing Ship Logistic) - Two orders for the replacement of the ageing LSLs SIR GERAINT and SIR PERCIVALE are anticipated.
RO-RO CONTAINER SHIPS - Four proposed under SDR are scheduled to be fully operational during 2000. They will either be new construction or chartered.
COASTAL SURVEY SHIPS - Three are urgently required to replace BULLDOG, BEAGLE and ROEBUCK.
NEW HOSPITAL SHIPS - Although two ships were proposed under SDR, the first will not enter service until 2005.

THE ROYAL FLEET AUXILIARY

The Royal Fleet Auxiliary Service (RFA) is a civilian manned fleet owned and operated by the Ministry of Defence. Its main task is to supply warships of the Royal Navy at sea with fuel, food, stores and ammunition which they need to remain operational while away from base. The service also provides aviation support and training facilities for the Royal Navy – together with amphibious support and secure sea transport for for the Royal Marines and British Army units.

The RFA is the largest single employer of UK merchant navy officers and ratings. Although the ethos is very much based on that of the Merchant Service, the personnel undergo a considerable overlay of naval training, in the main to provide them with a greater degree of survivability when operating their ships in hostile waters. Such training includes the operation and maintenance of close range and small calibre weapons and decoys (self-defence weapons), firefighting and damage control. But, fundamental to the success of the RFA is the need for competent seamen to undertake replenishment at sea and small boat operations, and to man ships flight decks to ensure the safe operation of helicopters.

The service prides itself that each ship is available for operations for approximately 80% of the year. Unlike the Royal Navy, officers and men of the RFA join a vessel for a period of time - say six months - and do not expect to be in port for leave periods at all during this period.

Throughout 1998 the Service maintained its standing commitment to provide tankers, giving vital support, in the West Indies, the Falklands and the Gulf. Additionally a tanker accompanied the West African Deployment Ship for most of this period. During the Gulf crisis earlier that year the carrier task groups were serviced with fuel, ammunition and stores by the "one-stop", AORs, FORT GEORGE and FORT VICTORIA.

With the RFA flotilla now containing a considerable number of old ships, maintenance problems are increasing. The arrival of the two new fleet tankers under construction at GEC Marine, along with two new landing ships is eagerly awaited. The recent Strategic Defence Review further offers the prospect of a further two strategic lift ships and a hospital ship for the RFA.

SHIPS OF THE ROYAL FLEET AUXILIARY
Pennant Numbers

Ship	Pennant Number	Ship	Pennant Number	Ship	Pennant Number
BRAMBLELEAF	A81	OLNA	A123	FORT VICTORIA	A387
SEA CRUSADER	A96	DILIGENCE	A132	FORT GEORGE	A388
SEA CHIEFTAN	A97	ARGUS	A135	SIR BEDIVERE	L3004
SEA CENTURION	A98	GREY ROVER	A269	SIR GALAHAD	L3005
BAYLEAF	A109	GOLD ROVER	A271	SIR GERAINT	L3027
ORANGELEAF	A110	BLACK ROVER	A273	SIR PERCIVALE	L3036
OAKLEAF	A111	FORT GRANGE	A385	SIR TRISTRAM	L3505
OLWEN	A122	FORT AUSTIN	A386		

● TERRY HOLTHAM

RFA Olna

'OL' CLASS

Ship	Pennant Number	Completion Date	Builder
OLWEN	A122	1965	Hawthorn Leslie
OLNA	A123	1966	Hawthorn Leslie

Displacement 36,000 tons **Dimensions** 197m x 26m x 10m **Speed** 19 knots **Complement** 92.

Notes

These Fast Fleet Tankers can operate up to 3 Sea King helicopters. Have been used for operational flying training of RN helicopter crews when ARGUS unavailable. Dry stores can be carried and transferred at sea, as well as a wide range of fuel, aviation spirits and lubricants. Both ships are due to be replaced by new-build auxiliary oilers (to be named WAVE KNIGHT (A389) and WAVE RULER (A390) curently under construction.

● OFFICIAL

RFA Gold Rover

ROVER CLASS

Ship	Pennant Number	Completion Date	Builder
GREY ROVER	A269	1970	Swan Hunter
GOLD ROVER ✓	A271	1974	Swan Hunter
BLACK ROVER	A273	1974	Swan Hunter

Displacement 11,522 tons **Dimensions** 141m x 19m x 7m **Speed** 18 knots **Armament** 2 - 20mm guns **Complement** 49/54

Notes

Small Fleet Tankers designed to supply warships with fresh water, dry cargo and refrigerated provisions, as well as a range of fuels and lubricants. Helicopter deck, but no hangar. Have been employed in recent years mainly as support for Falkland Islands and West Indies Guard ships, spending up to two years on deployment in these areas. There are currently no plans to replace these three ships.

● TERRY HOLTHAM

RFA Oakleaf

LEAF CLASS

Ship	Pennant Number	Completion Date	Builder
BRAMBLELEAF ✓	A81	1980	Cammell Laird
BAYLEAF	A109	1982	Cammell Laird
ORANGELEAF	A110	1982	Cammell Laird
OAKLEAF	A111	1981	Uddevalla V

Displacement 37,747 tons **Dimensions** 170m x 26m x 12m **Speed** 14.5 knots **Complement** 60.

Notes
All are ex merchant ships, originally acquired for employment mainly on freighting duties. All have been modified to enable them to refuel warships at sea. One of the class is normally permanently on station in the Gulf in support of Armilla Patrol and allied warships. BRAMBLELEAF is MOD(N) owned, the remainder on long-term bareboat charter. OAKLEAF differs from the other three ships, which are all commercial Stat32 tankers. At 49,310 tons displacement, she is still the largest vessel in RN/RFA service.

● D HANNAFORD

RFA Fort Grange

FORT CLASS I

Ship	Pennant Number	Completion Date	Builder
FORT GRANGE	A385	1978	Scott Lithgow
FORT AUSTIN	A386	1979	Scott Lithgow

Displacement 23,384 tons **Dimensions** 183m x 24m x 9m **Speed** 20 knots
Complement 201, (120 RFA, 36 RNSTS & 45 RN).

Notes
Full hangar and maintenance facilities are provided and up to four Sea King helicopters can be carried for both the transfer of stores and anti-submarine protection of a group of ships. Both ships can be armed with 4 - 20mm guns mounted on the Scot platforms. FORT GRANGE is alongside in Split, her role being to provide support to British Forces operating in the former Yugoslavia. She is expected to be renamed FORT ROSALIE in early 1999 to avoid confusion with FORT GEORGE.

● MARITIME PHOTOGRAPHIC

RFA Fort Victoria

FORT CLASS II

Ship	Pennant Number	Completion Date	Builder
FORT VICTORIA	A387	1992	Harland & Wolff
FORT GEORGE ✓	A388	1993	Swan Hunter

Displacement 31,500 tons **Dimensions** 204m x 30m x 9m **Speed** 20 knots **Armament** 4 - 30mm guns, 2 x Phalanx CIWS, Sea Wolf Missile System (Fitted for but not with) **Complement** 100 (RFA), 24 civilians, 32 RN and up to 122 aircrew.

Notes

"One stop" replenishment ships with the widest range of armaments, fuel and spares carried.Can operate up to 5 Sea King Helicopters with full maintenance facilities onboard. Both vessels eventually entered service after a series of delays in 1994. Flight deck facilities frequently used as training area for helicopter crews.

43

● OFFICIAL PHOTO

RFA Sir Bedivere

LANDING SHIPS (LOGISTIC)
SIR LANCELOT CLASS

Ship	Pennant Number	Completion Date	Builder
SIR BEDIVERE ✓	L3004	1967	Hawthorn
SIR GALAHAD	L3005	1987	Swan Hunter
SIR GERAINT	L3027	1967	Stephen
SIR PERCIVALE	L3036	1968	Hawthorn
SIR TRISTRAM	L3505	1967	Hawthorn

Displacement 5,550 tons **Dimensions** 126m x 18m x 4m **Speed** 17 knots **Armament** Can be fitted with 20 or 40mm guns in emergency **Complement** 65, (SIR GALAHAD is larger at 8,451 tons. 140m x 20m **Complement** 58).

Notes
Manned by the RFA but tasked by the Army, these ships are used for heavy secure transport of stores – embarked by bow and stern doors – and beach assault landings. Can operate helicopters from both vehicle and flight deck if required and carry 340 troops. SIR TRISTRAM was rebuilt after extensive Falklands War damage. After extensive delays, SIR BEDIVERE completed a Ship Life Extension Programme (SLEP) at Rosyth in 1998. She is now 7,700 tonnes displacement and her dimensions are 137 x 20 x 4 metres.

● TERRY HOLTHAM

RFA Sea Crusader

Ship	Pennant Number	Completion Date	Builder
SEA CRUSADER	A96	1996	Kawasaki Heavy Industries

Displacement 25,500 tonnes **Dimensions** 164m x 25m x 6.5m **Speed** 18 knots **Complement** 17

Notes

A commercial Roll on-Roll off cargo ship, chartered while under construction in Japan. Arrived in UK in November 1996, her main role being a heavy-lift ship for the Joint Rapid Reaction Force. Routinely employed on freighting runs transporting armoured vehicles and equipment to Split, and continental ports. 2,500 lane metres of vehicle capacity available. Originally due to be returned to her owners in October, 1998 her MoD charter has however been extended to April 1999.

● MARITIME PHOTOGRAPHIC

RFA Sea Centurion

Ship	Pennant Number	Completion Date	Builder
SEA CENTURION	A 98	1998	Societa Esercizio Cantieri

Displacement 21,000 tonnes **Dimensions** 183m x 26m x 7m **Speed** 22 knots
Complement 18

Notes

First of class of a new generation of Ro-Ro ships, Stena 4-runner class on bareboat charter from Stena from new-build, initially for 18 months with options to extend. Joined the RFA in October 98 for service with the JRDF. Routine use will be for freighting military vehicles and equipment. 2715 lane metres on three cargo decks, accessed by a large stern tamp and internal ramps. Similarly a chartered sister ship SEA CHIEFTAIN (A97) the second of class, is expected to join the RFA in April 1999.

● OFFICIAL PHOTO

RFA Diligence

Ship	Pennant Number	Completion Date	Builder
DILIGENCE	A132	1981	Oesundsvarvet

Displacement 5,814 tons **Dimensions** 120m x 12m x 3m **Speed** 15 knots **Armament** 2 - 20mm **Complement** RFA 40, RN Personnel – approx 100.

Notes

Formerly the M/V STENA INSPECTOR purchased (£25m) for service in the South Atlantic. Her deep diving complex was removed and workshops added. Has given valuable support to a wide range of warships in the Falklands and Gulf but now operates additionally with a 'worldwide' role for submarine and MCMV support.

● OFFICIAL PHOTO

RFA Argus

Ship	Pennant Number	Completion Date	Builder
ARGUS	A135	1981	Cantieri Navali Breda

Displacement 28,081 tons (full load) **Dimensions** 175m x 30m x 8m **Speed** 18 knots **Armament** 4 - 30 mm, 2 - 20 mm **Complement** 254 (inc 137 Air Group) **Aircraft** 6 Sea King, 12 Harriers can be carried in a "ferry role".

Notes

Formerly the M/V CONTENDER BEZANT taken up from trade during the Falklands crisis. Purchased in 1984 (£13 million) for conversion to an 'Aviation Training Ship'. A £50 million re-build was undertaken at Belfast from 1984-87. Undertook rapid conversion in October 1990 to "Primary Casualty Reception Ship" (Hospital Ship!) for service in the Gulf. These facilities remain "mothballed" on board for activation if required.

David Hannaford

HMS OCEAN

A J Holtham

HMS LIVERPOOL

F236

HMS MONTROSE

Mike Welsford

Maritime Photographic

HMS ANGLESEY

T G Holtham

M39

HMS HURWORTH

RFA ORANGELEAF

T G Holtham

ORANGELEAF

Maritime Photographic

ADEPT

RFA SIR GALAHAD

L3005

T G Holtham

ROYAL MARITIME
AUXILIARY SERVICE

The Naval Bases and Supply Agency (NBSA) is responsible for the provision of Out-of-Port and In-Port maritime services in support of: Naval Bases, CinC Fleet, The Meteorological Office, Defence, Evaluation and Research Agency (DERA), RAF and Army. In addition, NBSA undertakes through Marine Services: Mooring and Navigation buoy maintenance, freighting of Naval armaments and explosives, maritime support to the DERA underwater research programme and sea-borne services to the Fleet. Maritime services at the Kyle of Lochalsh are provided primarily to support the British Underwater Test and Evaluation Centre (BUTEC) Ranges, and secondarily to fulfil Fleet requirements in that area. The Director Base Support (DBS) is tasked by NBSA with the provision of these Marine Services.

In the three main Ports at Portsmouth, Devonport and Clyde the service is currently delivered under a Government Owned/Commercially Operated (GOCO) contract with SERCo-Denholm Ltd. The vessels being operated on a Bare Boat Charter basis.

For Naval Armament Freighting, Mooring Maintenance, RMAS NEWTON and services at the Kyle of Lochalsh, the service is currently delivered under Service Level Agreement (SLA) by the General Manager RMAS from his HQ at Pembroke Dock.

For both RAF training and Range Safety Clearance duties at Army and MoD ranges throughout Britain, services are currently delivered under two separate Government Owned/Commercially Operated (GOCO) contracts. Management of these contracts and overall provision of the service remains the responsibility of DBS.

Marine Services vessels can be seen at work in the UK Naval Bases and are easily identified by their black hulls, buff coloured superstructure and by their Flag, which in the case of GM RMAS vessels, is a blue ensign defaced in the fly by a yellow anchor over two wavy lines. The remaining vessels fly the 'Other Government Vessels' ensign. Which is a blue ensign defaced in the fly by a yellow anchor.

SHIPS OF
THE ROYAL MARITIME AUXILIARY SERVICE
Pennant Numbers

Ship	Pennant Number	Ship	Pennant Number
CAMERON	A72	NORAH	A205
MELTON	A83	LAMLASH	A208
MENAI	A84	LECHLADE	A211
MEON	A87	BEE	A216
MILFORD	A91	FORCEFUL	A221
CAIRN	A126	NIMBLE	A222
TORRENT	A127	POWERFUL	A223
DALMATIAN	A129	ADEPT	A224
TORNADO	A140	BUSTLER	A225
TORCH	A141	CAPABLE	A226
TORMENTOR	A142	CAREFUL	A227
WATERMAN	A146	FAITHFUL	A228
FRANCES	A147	COCKCHAFER	A230
FIONA	A148	DEXTEROUS	A231
FLORENCE	A149	ADAMANT	A232
GENEVIEVE	A150	SHEEPDOG	A250
KITTY	A170	LADYBIRD	A253
LESLEY	A172	ILCHESTER	A308
LILAH	A174	INSTOW	A309
HUSKY	A178	IXWORTH	A318
MASTIFF	A180	COLLIE	A328
SALUKI	A182	IMPULSE	A344
SALMOOR	A185	IMPETUS	A345
SALMASTER	A186	ELKSTONE	A353
SALMAID	A187	EPWORTH	A355
SETTER	A189	NEWTON	A367
JOAN	A190	WARDEN	A368
BOVISAND	A191	KINTERBURY	A378
CAWSAND	A192	ARROCHAR	A382
HELEN	A198	APPLEBY	A383
MYRTLE	A199	DUNSTER	A393
SPANIEL	A201	GRASMERE	A402

Ship	Pennant Number	Ship	Pennant Number
HEADCORN	A1766	FALCONET	Y01
HEVER	A1767	PETARD	Y02
HARLECH	A1768	OILPRESS	Y21
HAMBLEDON	A1769	MOORHEN	Y32
HOLMWOOD	A1772	MOORFOWL	Y33
HORNING	A1773		

KEEP UP TO DATE
THROUGHOUT THE YEAR

Warship World is published each quarter and gives you all the information necessary to keep this book updated throughout the year. See inside front cover for details.

This book is updated and re-issued every *December*. Keep up to date … Don't miss the new edition.

Phone 01579 343663 for details.

●TERRY HOLTHAM

MV Impetus

IMPULSE CLASS

Ship	Pennant Number	Completion Date	Builder
IMPULSE	A344	1993	Dunston
IMPETUS	A345	1993	Dunston

G.R.T. 400 tons approx **Dimensions** 33m x 10m x 4m **Speed** 12 knots
Complement 5.

Notes
Completed in 1993 specifically to serve as berthing tugs for the Trident Class submarines at Faslane. Both operated under contract by Serco Denholm.

● CHRIS ROGERS

MV Powerful

HARBOUR TUGS
TWIN UNIT TRACTOR TUGS (TUTT'S)

Ship	Pennant Number	Completion Date	Builder
FORCEFUL ✓	A221	1985	R. Dunston
NIMBLE	A222	1985	R. Dunston
POWERFUL	A223	1985	R. Dunston
ADEPT ✓	A224	1980	R. Dunston
BUSTLER	A225	1981	R. Dunston
CAPABLE	A226	1981	R. Dunston
CAREFUL ✓	A227	1982	R. Dunston
FAITHFUL ✓	A228	1985	R. Dunston
DEXTEROUS	A231	1986	R. Dunston

G.R.T. 375 tons **Dimensions** 39m x 10m x 4m **Speed** 12 knots **Complement** 9.

Notes
The principal harbour tugs in naval service. All operated under contract by Serco Denholm except CAPABLE at Gibraltar which is managed locally.

61

● D HANNAFORD

MV Mastiff

DOG CLASS

Ship	Pennant Number	Ship	Pennant Number
CAIRN ●	A126	SETTER	A189
DALMATIAN	A129	SPANIEL	A201
HUSKY	A178	SHEEPDOG	A250
MASTIFF	A180	COLLIE ●	A328
SALUKI	A182		

G.R.T. 152 tons **Dimensions** 29m x 8m x 4m **Speed** 12 knots **Complement** 5.

Notes
General harbour tugs – all completed between 1965 and 1969. All except those marked ● are operated by Serco Denholm. COLLIE and CAIRN are no longer tugs but are classified as trials vessels - based at Kyle of Lochalsh.

● MARITIME PHOTOGRAPHIC

MV Kitty

TRITON CLASS

Ship	Pennant Number	Ship	Pennant Number
KITTY	A170	JOAN	A190
LESLEY	A172	MYRTLE	A199
LILAH	A174	NORAH	A205

G.R.T. 89 tons **Speed** 8 knots **Complement** 4.

Notes
Known as Water Tractors these craft are used for basin moves and towage of light barges. Operated by Serco Denholm Ltd.

● D HANNAFORD

MV Florence

FELICITY CLASS

Ship	Pennant Number	Ship	Pennant Number
FRANCES	A147	FLORENCE	A149
FIONA	A148	GENEVIEVE	A150
HELEN	A198		

G.R.T. 80 tons **Speed** 10 knots **Complement** 4.

Notes
Water Tractors used for the movement of small barges and equipment. All are operated by Serco Denholm. Two sister vessels (GEORGINA and GWENDOLINE) sold to Serco Denholm in 1996 for service in H M Naval bases. (Both now painted red/pink).

● D HANNAFORD

RMAS Newton

RESEARCH VESSEL

Ship	Pennant Number	Completion Date	Builder
NEWTON ⌇	A367	1976	Scotts

G.R.T. 2,779 tons **Dimensions** 99m x 16m x 6m **Speed** 15 knots **Complement** 29

Notes
Primarily used in the support of RN training exercises. Some limited support provided to DERA trials. Cable laying capability retained. Operated by the RMAS.

● D HANNAFORD

RMAS Kinterbury

NAVAL ARMAMENT VESSELS

Ship	Pennant Number	Completion Date	Builder
KINTERBURY	A378	1981	Appledore SB
ARROCHAR	A382	1981	Appledore SB

G.R.T. 1,357 tons **Dimensions** 64m x 12m x 5m **Speed** 14 knots **Complement** 11.

Notes

Two holds carry Naval armament stores, ammunition and guided missiles. Both vessels vary slightly. ARROCHAR (ex ST GEORGE) taken over in late 1988 from the Army. Both vessels continue to be operated by the RMAS. In addition to freighting tasks they are also used for trials work and in support of RN exercises.

● MARITIME PHOTOGRAPHIC

MV Ladybird

INSECT CLASS

Ship	Pennant Number	Completion Date	Builder
BEE	A216	1970	C.D. Holmes
COCKCHAFER	A230	1973	Beverley
LADYBIRD	A253	1973	Beverley

G.R.T. 279 tons **Dimensions** 34m x 8m x 3m **Speed** 10.5 knots **Complement** 7-9.

Notes
COCKCHAFER is fitted as a Trials Stores Carrier and operated by the RMAS at Kyle of Lochalsh. She will be withdrawn in early 1999 and replaced by WARDEN. LADY-BIRD is a Naval Armament carrier and operated by Serco Denholm. BEE is operated by AV Seawork.

● MARITIME PHOTOGRAPHIC

MV Cawsand

Ship	Pennant Number	Completion Date	Builder
BOVISAND	A191	1997	FBM (Cowes)
CAWSAND	A192	1997	FBM (Cowes)

G.R.T 225 tonnes **Dimensions** 23m x 11m x 2m **Speed** 15 knots **Complement** 5

Notes

These craft are used in support of Flag Officer Sea Training (FOST) at Plymouth to transfer staff quickly and comfortably to and from Warships and Auxiliaries within and beyond the Plymouth breakwater in open sea condition. These are the first vessels of a small waterplane area twin hull (SWATH) design to be ordered by the Ministry of Defence and cost £6.5 million.

● LEO VAN GINDEREN MV Adamant

ADAMANT

Ship	Pennant Number	Completion Date	Builder
ADAMANT	A232	1992	FBM (Cowes)

G.R.T 170 tonnes **Dimensions** 30m x 8m x 1m **Speed** 22 knots **Complement** 5

Notes
Twin catamaran hulls based on the commercial Red Jet design (as used by Red Funnel Ferry Co). First water jet propulsion vessel owned by MoD(N). In service as a Clyde personnel ferry - operated by Serco Denholm.

(TYPE A, B & X) TENDERS

Ship	Pennant Number	Ship	Pennant Number
MELTON	A83	ELKSTONE	A353
MENAI	A84	EPWORTH	A355
MEON	A87	DUNSTER	A393
MILFORD	A91	GRASMERE	A402
LAMLASH	A208	HEADCORN	A1766
LECHLADE	A211	HEAVER	A1767
ILCHESTER •	A308	HARLECH	A1768
INSTOW •	A309	HAMBLEDON	A1769
IRONBRIDGE •	A311	HOLMWOOD	A1772
IXWORTH •	A318	HORNING	A1773

G.R.T. 78 tons **Dimensions** 24m x 6m x 3m **Speed** 10.5 knots **Complement** 4/5.

Notes
Vessels marked • are diving tenders. Remainder are Training Tenders, Passenger Ferries, or Cargo Vessels. All except MELTON are operated by Serco Denholm. IRONBRIDGE and IXWORTH are RN manned. MEAVEY (SULTAN VENTURER), ELKSTONE, EPWORTH and GRASEMERE for sale in 1999.

● DANE MURDOCH

MV Oilpress

COASTAL OILERS
OILPRESS CLASS

Ship	Pennant Number	Completion Date	Builder
OILPRESS	Y21	1969	Appledore Shipbuilders

G.R.T. 362 tons **Dimensions** 41m x 9m x 3m **Speed** 11 knots **Complement** 5.

Notes
Employed as Harbour and Coastal Oiler. Operated by Serco Denholm. OILWELL and OILMAN sold in 1998.

MV Waterman

WATER CARRIERS
WATER CLASS

Ship	Pennant Number	Completion Date	Builder
WATERMAN	A146	1978	R. Dunston

G.R.T. 263 tons **Dimensions** 40m x 8m x 2m **Speed** 11 knots **Complement** 5.

Notes
Capable of coastal passages, these craft normally supply either demineralised or fresh water to the Fleet within port limits. WATERFOWL is owned and operated by Serco Denholm. WATERCOURSE sold in 1998.

72

● C. HOCKADAY

RMAS Torrent

TORPEDO RECOVERY VESSEL (TRV)
TORRID CLASS

Ship	Pennant Number	Completion Date	Builder
TORRENT	A127	1971	Cleland SB Co

G.R.T. 550 tons **Dimensions** 46m x 9m x 3m **Speed** 12 knots **Complement** 14.

Notes
A stern ramp is built for the recovery of torpedoes fired for trials and exercises. A total of 32 can be carried. Operated by the RMAS at Kyle of Lochalsh but will be replaced by WARDEN in 1999.

● D HANNAFORD

MV Tormentor

TORNADO CLASS

Ship	Pennant Number	Completion Date	Builder
TORNADO	A140	1979	Hall Russell
TORCH	A141	1980	Hall Russell
TORMENTOR	A142	1980	Hall Russell

G.R.T. 560 tons **Dimensions** 47m x 8m x 3m **Speed** 14 knots **Complement** 13.

Notes
All vessels have had suitable rails fitted to enable them to operate as exercise minelayers in addition to their torpedo recovery role. TORCH in reserve - future undecided. TOREADOR sold in 1998.

● W SARTORI

RMAS Salmoor

MOORING & SALVAGE VESSELS
SAL CLASS

Ship	Pennant Number	Completion Date	Builder
SALMOOR	A185	1985	Hall Russell
SALMASTER	A186	1986	Hall Russell
SALMAID	A187	1986	Hall Russell

Displacement 2200 tonnes **Dimensions** 77m x 15m x 4m **Speed** 15 knots **Complement** 19

Notes
Multi-purpose vessels designed to lay and maintain underwater targets, navigation marks and moorings. SALMASTER operated by Serco Denholm.

75

●DAVE CULLEN

MV Moorhen

MOOR CLASS

Ship	Pennant Number	Completion Date	Builder
MOORHEN	Y32	1989	McTay Marine
MOORFOWL	Y33	1989	McTay Marine
CAMERON	A72	1991	Richard Dunston

Displacement 518 tons **Dimensions** 32m x 11m x 2m **Speed** 8 knots **Complement** 10

Notes
Powered mooring lighters for use within sheltered coastal waters. CAMERON is similar but was sold to DERA at Dunfermline in 1996 and is employed as an Underwater Trials & Experimental vessel at Rosyth. Operated by Briggs Marine on behalf of DERA. MOORHEN based at Portsmouth and MOORFOWL at Devonport. Both vessels also undertake coastal work.

● D HANNAFORD

MV Warden

WARDEN CLASS

Ship	Pennant Number	Completion Date	Builder
WARDEN	A368	1989	Richards

Displacement 626 tons **Dimensions** 48m x 10m x 4m **Speed** 15 knots **Complement** 11.

Notes
Built as a Range Maintenance Vessel but will be based at Kyle of Lochalsh and operated by the RMAS in support of BUTEC when a Falmouth refit is completed in 1999.

The primary tasks for RAF Support craft include target towing, winch training helicopter crews for SAR and the vessels are also used for sea survival training of aircrew. Details of RAF Support Craft are as follows: (Vessels on this page are operated under contract by GFE AV Seawork)

LONG RANGE RECOVERY AND SUPPORT CRAFT (LRRSC)

Ship	Pennant Number	Completion Date	Builder
SEAL	5000	1967	Brooke Marine
SEAGULL	5001	1970	Fairmile Const.

G.R.T. 251 tons **Dimensions** 36.6m x 7.16mx 1.8m **Speed** 21 knots **Complement** 8. Both are based at Invergordon.

RESCUE AND TARGET TOWING LAUNCHES (RTTL)

SPITFIRE, HALIFAX, HAMPDEN, HURRICANE, LANCASTER & WELLINGTON

G.R.T. 60 tons **Dimensions** 24m x 5.6m x 1.6m **Speed** 21 knots **Complement** 4/6 They are based at Great Yarmouth and Plymouth.

There are also 3 x 63' Pinnaces Nos 1374, 1389 & 1392.
These 63' craft are employed on target towing, SAR training, sea survival drills & various trials and weapon recovery. They are based at Holyhead & Plymouth.

Details of Range Safety Craft are as follows:

Ship	Pennant Number	Completion Date	Builder
FALCONET	Y01	1983	James & Stone
PETARD	Y02	1978	James & Stone

G.R.T. 60 tons **Dimensions** 24m x 5.5m x 1.5m **Speed** 21 knots **Complement** 6. They are based at Benbecula and Pembroke Dock and operated by Smit International.

● DAVID HANNAFORD

HMAV Arakan

ARMY LANDING CRAFT
LCL CLASS (LANDING CRAFT LOGISTIC)

Vessel	Pennant Number	Completion Date	Builder
ARDENNES	L4001	1977	Brooke Marine
ARAKAN	L4003	1978	Brooke Marine

G.R.T. 1,595 tons **Dimensions** 72m x 15m x 4m **Speed** 10 knots **Complement** 35.

Notes
The Army's two LCLs (ARDENNES and ARAKAN) are designed for amphibious delivery of stores and material. They have a beaching capability, with a bow ramp to allow vehicles to drive on or off. The vessels can carry 356 tonnes of stores, or 36 ISO containers or 5 tanks or 118-ton trucks. Both are due to end their Army service in April 1999 as a result of the 1998 SDR cuts.

● MARITIME PHOTOGRAPHIC

RCTV Aachen

RCL CLASS
(RAMPED CRAFT LOGISTIC)

Vessel	Pennant Number	Completion Date	Builder
ARROMANCHES	L105	1987	James & Stone
ANDALSNES	L107	1984	James & Stone
AKYAB	L109	1984	James & Stone
AACHEN	L110	1986	James & Stone
AREZZO	L111	1986	James & Stone
AUDEMER	L113	1987	James & Stone

Displacement 165 tons **Dimensions** 33m x 8m x 1.5m **Speed** 9 knots
Complement 6.

Notes
Smaller – "all purpose" landing craft capable of carrying up to 96 tons. In service in coastal waters around Cyprus and UK. ARROMANCHES was formerly AGHEILA (re-named 1994 when original vessel was sold).

• CHRIS ROGERS   Appleby

SEA CADET VESSELS

FLEET TENDERS 63 DESIGN

Ship	Pennant Number	Ship	Pennant Number
ALNMOUTH	Y13	APPLEBY	A383

Displacement 117 tons **Dimensions** 24m x 5m x 3m **Speed** 10.5 knots.

Notes
Craft are loaned by MoD to the Sea Cadet Corps and were used by units throughout the UK.from March to October each year. Accommodation for 12 cadets and up to 8 adults. Both vessels were returned to MoD on 9 November 1998 for commercial sale.

Ex-BIBURY (A103) operates for Portsmouth Naval Base Sub Aqua Club.

AIRCRAFT OF THE FLEET AIR ARM

THE SHAPE OF THINGS TO COME

The Merlin HM Mk 1 is the replacement for the anti-submarine Sea King HAS Mk 6. It is the first Royal Naval derivative of the EH101 helicopter, designed and produced under a collaborative programme by UK's GKN Westland Helicopters Ltd and Italy's helicopter manufacturer, Agusta. A highly complex and advanced aircraft, the ultimate manufacture of the Merlin HM Mk 1 weapon system is taking place under the Prime Contractorship of Lockheed Martin ASIC.

Flown normally by a crew of 3 (1 x Pilot, 1 x Observer, 1 x Aircrewman), Merlin was designed to operate from both large and small ship's flight decks, in severe weather and high sea states, by day and night.

Powered by three Rolls Royce Turbomeca gas turbines and with a maximum all-up-mass of 14,600 kgs, and a top speed of 150 kts, the Merlin can carry four homing torpedoes or depth charges, and has sufficient fuel for a radius of operation of over 200 nautical miles.

The first Merlin Intensive Flying Trials Unit (700M Naval Air Squadron) commissioned at RNAS CULDROSE on 1 December 1998. It is expected that the first front line squadron and Type 23 frigate Flights will be ready to deploy early in 2001.

British Aerospace Sea Harrier

Variants: FA2
Role: Short take off, vertical landing (STOVL) fighter attack and reconnaissance aircraft.
Engine: 1 x 21,500lb thrust Rolls Royce PEGASUS 104, turbofan.
Span 25' 3" **Length** 49' 1" **Height** 12' 0" **Max weight** 26,200lb.
Max speed Mach .9 540 knots **Crew** 1 pilot.
Avionics: Blue Vixen pulse doppler radar
Armament: Up to 4 x AMRAAM Air to Air Missiles. SEA EAGLE air to surface missiles. SIDEWINDER air to air missiles. 2 - 30mm Aden cannons with 120 rounds per gun in detachable pods, one either side of the lower fuselage. 1 fuselage centreline and 4 underwing hardpoints. The inner wing stations are capable of carrying 2,000lb of stores and are plumbed for drop tanks. The other positions can carry stores up to 1,000lb in weight. Possible loads include 1,000lb or practice bombs; BL 755 cluster bombs, 190 or 100 gallon drop tanks. A single F95 camera is mounted obliquely in the nose for reconnaissance.
Squadron Service: 800, 801 and 899 squadrons in commission.
Notes: During 1999, 800 squadron will be embarked in HMS INVINCIBLE and 801 in HMS ILLUSTRIOUS. 899 squadron is responsible for the training of pilots and maintainers and the development of tactics. It is normally shore based at Yeovilton. In a period of tension it could embark to reinforce the embarked air groups in the carriers.

MARITIME PHOTOGRAPHIC

Westland SEA KING

Developed for the Royal Navy from the Sikorsky SH3D, the basic Sea King airframe is used in three different roles. The following details are common to all:
Engines: 2 x 1600shp Rolls Royce Gnome H 1400 – 1 free power turbines.
Rotor Diameter 62' 0" **Length** 54' 9" **Height** 17' 2" **Max Weight** 21,400lb **Max Speed** 125 knots.
The 3 versions are:-

MARITIME PHOTOGRAPHIC

SAR MK 5 : HAS 6

The HAS6 has improved sonics, deeper dipping active sonar and ESM
Roles: Anti-submarine search and attack. SAR. Transport.
Crew: 2 pilots, 1 observer and 1 aircrewman.
Avionics: Sea Searcher radar; Type 2069 variable depth active/passive sonar AQS 902 passive sonobuoy analyser. Orange Crop passive ESM equipment.
Armament: 4 fuselage hardpoints capable of carrying STINGRAY torpedoes or depth charges. Various flares, markers, grenades and sonobuoys can be carried internally and hand launched. A 7.62mm machine gun can be mounted in the doorway.
Squadron Service: 771 Squadron operates an SAR 5. 810, 814, 819, and 820 squadrons are in commission equipped with HAS 6.
Notes: The Sea King has been the backbone of the Fleet Air Arm's anti-submarine force since 1970. 810 squadron at Culdrose provides advanced and operational flying training, with the capability to embark to reinforce the front line. During 1999, 814 squadron will be embarked in HMS INVINCIBLE and 820 in HMS ILLUSTRIOUS. 819 is shore based at Prestwick The SAR 5 has an excellent SAR capability which is frequently demonstrated in the south west approaches. The HAS 6 has less complete SAR facilities when full ASW equipment fitted.

84

● OFFICIAL PHOTO

AEW 2

Role: Airborne Early Warning. **Crew:** 1 pilot and 2 observers.
Avionics: Thorn/EMI Searchwater radar Orange Crop passive ESM equipment.
Squadron Service: 849 HQ, 849A and 849B Flights in commission.
Notes: Used to detect low flying aircraft trying to attack aircraft carrier battle groups under conventional shipborne radar cover. Can also be used for surface search utilising its sophisticated, computerised long range radar. During 1999 849A Flight will be embarked in HMS INVINCIBLE and 849B Flight in HMS ILLUSTRIOUS. 849HQ acts as a training and trials unit at Culdrose.

● OFFICIAL PHOTO

HC 4

Role: Commando assault and utility transport.
Crew: 2 pilots and 1 aircrewman.
Armament: Door mounted 7.62mm machine gun.
Squadron Service: 845, 846 and 848 squadrons in commission.
Notes: The HC4 has a fixed undercarriage with no sponsons or radome.Can carry up to 27 troops in the cabin or underslung loads up to 6,000lb in weight. All squadrons are based at Yeovilton but embark or detach at short notice to support 3 Cdo Brigade. 845 Sqn has had aircraft based in Split in support of UN and NATO Forces in Bosnia since1993.

● OFFICIAL PHOTO

Westland LYNX

Variants: HAS 3, HAS 3S, HMA 8.
Roles: Surface search and attack; anti-submarine attack; SAR; troop carrying.
Engines: 2 x 900hp Rolls Royce GEM BS 360-07-26 free shaft turbines.
Rotor diameter: 42' 0" **Length** 39' 1" **Height** 11' 0" **Max Weight** 9,500lb.
Max Speed: 150 knots. **Crew:** 1 pilot and 1 observer.
Avionics: SEA SPRAY radar. Orange Crop passive ESM equipment. Sea Owl PID (Mk 8)
Armament: External pylons carry up to 4 - SEA SKUA air to surface missiles or 2 x STINGRAY torpedoes, depth charges and markers.
Squadron Service: 702 and 815 squadrons in commission.

Notes: 815 OEU is a trials Flight for HMA 8 Mk8 aircraft. 702 is the training squadron . 815 squadron is the parent unit for single aircraft ships flights. Both squadrons move from Portland to Yeovilton in January 1999.
All ships' flight aircraft are being converted to HMA Mk8 specification. Full delivery of 59 conversions are expected by 2003.
Another version of the Lynx, the AH7, is operated by Royal Marines in 847 NAS.

● OFFICIAL PHOTO

Westland GAZELLE AH 1

Engine: 1 x 592shp Turbomeca ASTAZOU free power turbine.
Crew: 1 or 2 pilots.

Notes: The Gazelle AH1 is used by 847 NAS based at Yeovilton as a spotter/commu-
nications aircraft for the Royal Marines.

OTHER AIRCRAFT TYPES IN ROYAL NAVY SERVICE DURING 1999

British Aerospace JETSTREAM T2 and T3

Engines: 2 x 940hp Turbomeca ASTAZOU 16D turboprops. (T3 Garrett turboprops).
Crew: 1 or 2 pilots, 2 student observers plus 3 other seats.
Notes: T2's are used by 750 squadron at Culdrose for training Fleet Air Arm Observers.T3's are used by the Heron flight at Yeovilton for operational support/communications flying.

● OFFICIAL PHOTO

British Aerospace HAWK

Engine: 1 x Ardour Mk 151 5200 lbs thrust.
Crew: 1 or 2 Pilots (both service and civilian)
Notes: With FRADU at Culdrose to provide support for training of RN ships, RN flying standards flight and as airborne targets for the aircraft direction school.

● OFFICIAL PHOTO

GROB G115 D-2

Has taken over the flying grading and conversion of Rotary to Fixed Wing flying task from the Chipmunk. They are owned and operated by a division of Short Brothers plc. They operate from Plymouth City Airport.

Royal Navy Historic Flight

The RNHF is supported financially by the Swordfish Heritage Trust. The Historic Flight has been civilianised since 1993.

The current holding of aircraft is:

Flying: 2 Fairey Swordfish, 1 Fairey Firefly (Overhaul 1998/9),1 Sea Hawk (under repair), 1 Sea Fury.
Static Display: 1 Fairey Swordfish

Full details of these and many other naval aircraft can be found in the revised edition of AIRCRAFT OF THE ROYAL NAVY SINCE 1945 published by Maritime Books.

WEAPONS OF THE ROYAL NAVY
Sea Launched Missiles

Trident II D5

The American built Lockheed Martin Trident 2 (D5) submarine launched strategic missiles are Britain's only nuclear weapons and form the UK contribution to the NATO strategic deterrent. 16 missiles, each capable of carrying up to 6 UK manufactured thermonuclear warheads (but currently limited to 4 under current government policy), are aboard each of the Vanguard class SSBNs. Trident has a maximum range of 12,000 km and is powered by a three stage rocket motor. Launch weight is 60 tonnes, overall length and width are 13.4 metres and 2.1 metres respectively.

Sea Wolf

Short range rapid reaction anti-missile and anti-aircraft weapon. The complete weapon system, including radars and fire control computers, is entirely automatic in operation. Type 22 frigates carry two sextuple Sea Wolf launchers but the subsequent Type 23 frigates carry 32 Vertical Launch Seawolf (VLS) in a silo on the foredeck. Basic missile data: weight 82 kg, length 1.9 m, wingspan 56 cm, range c.56 km, warhead 13.4 kg. The VLS missile is basically similar but has jettisonable tandem boost rocket motors.

Harpoon

The Boeing (McDonnell Douglas) Harpoon is a sophisticated anti-ship missile using a combination of inertial guidance and active radar homing to attack targets out to a range of 130 km, cruising at Mach 0.9 and carrying a 227 kg warhead. Currently fitted to the Batch II Type 22 and Type 23 frigates. It is powered by a lightweight turbojet but is accelerated at launch by a booster rocket. The Royal Navy also deploys the UGM-84 submarine launched version aboard its Swiftsure and Trafalgar class SSNs.

Sea Dart

A medium range area defence anti aircraft missile powered by a ramjet and solid fuel booster rocket. Maximum effective range is in the order of 80 km and the missile accelerates to a speed of Mach 3.5. It forms the main armament of the Type 42 destroyers and was originally fitted to the Invincible class carriers. Missile weight 550 kg, length 4.4 m, wingspan 0.91 m.

Exocet (MM38)

A French developed medium range sea skimming anti ship missile powered by a two stage rocket motor giving it a maximum range of 45 km at a speed of Mach 0.93 carrying a 165 kg blast and fragmentation warhead. Although extensively deployed in the past, it is now only carried by the remaining Batch II Type 22 frigates. Weight 750 kg, length 5.21 m, wingspan 1 m.

Tomahawk (BGM-109)

This is a land attack cruise missile with a range of 1600 km and can be launched from a variety of platforms including surface ships and submarines. Some 65 of the latter version were purchased from America to arm Trafalgar class SSNs with the first being delivered to the Royal Navy for trials during 1998. Tomahawk is fired in a disposal container from the submarine's conventional torpedo tubes and is then accelerated to its subsonic cruising speed by a booster rocket motor before a lightweight F-107 turbojet takes over for the cruise. Its extremely accurate guidance system means that small targets can be hit with precision at maximum range, as was dramatically illustrated in the Gulf War. Total weight of the submarine version, including its launch capsule is 1816 kg, it carries a 450 kg warhead, length is 6.4 metres and wingspan (fully extended) 2.54 m.

Air Launched Missiles

Sea Skua

A small anti ship missile developed by British Aerospace arming the Lynx helicopters carried by various frigates and destroyers. The missile weighs 147 kg, has a length of 2.85 m and a span of 62 cm. Powered by solid fuel booster and sustainer rocket motors, it has a range of over 15 km at high subsonic speed. Sea Skua is particularly effective against patrol vessels and fast attack craft, as was demonstrated in both the Falklands and Gulf Wars.

Sea Eagle

A highly effective anti-ship missile carrying a 230 kg warhead over a range of 110 km. Also designed and manufactured by British Aerospace, Sea Eagle is powered by a small turbo-fan engine and uses a combination of inertial guidance and an active radar seeker to find its target. Weight is 600 kg, length 4.15 m and wingspan 1.2 m. It entered service in 1985, equipping maritime strike aircraft of the RAF as well as the Navy's Sea Harriers.

Sidewinder

This is one of the world's most successful short range air to air missiles. The latest AIM-9L version carried by Sea Harriers uses a heat seeking infra red guidance system and has a range of 18 km. Powered by a solid fuel rocket motor boosting it to speeds of Mach 2.5, it weighs 86.6 kg and is 2.87 m long.

AMRAAM

The Hughes AIM-120 Advanced Medium Range Air To Air Missile arms the latest Sea Harrier FA.2 and has a range of around 50 km. Weight 157 kg, length 3.65 m. Coupled with the Blue Vixen multi mode radar, the AMRAAM gives a substantial boost to the aircraft's capability as an air defence interceptor, allowing Beyond Visual Range (BVR) engagements.

Guns

114mm Vickers Mk8

The Royal Navy's standard medium calibre general purpose gun which arms the later Type 22s, Type 23 frigates and Type 42 destroyers. Rate of fire: 25 rounds/min. Range: 22,000 m. Weight of Shell: 21 kg.

Goalkeeper

A highly effective automatic Close in Weapons System (CIWS) designed to shoot down missiles and aircraft which have evaded the outer layers of a ships defences. The complete system, designed and built in Holland, is on an autonomous mounting and includes radars, fire control computers and a 7-barrel 30 mm Gatling gun firing 4200 rounds/min. Goalkeeper is designed to engage targets between 350 and 1500 metres away.

Phalanx

A US built CIWS designed around the Vulcan 20 mm rotary cannon. Rate of fire is 3000 rounds/min and effective range is c.1500 m. Fitted in Type 42, HM Ships OCEAN and FEARLESS.

GCM-AO3 30mm

This mounting carries two Oerlikon 30 mm guns each capable of firing 650 rounds/min. Effective range is 3000 m. Fitted to Type 22 frigates and the LPDs.

DS30B 30mm

Single 30 mm mounting carrying an Oerlikon 30 mm gun. Fitted to Type 23 frigates and various patrol vessels and MCMVs.

GAM BO 20 mm

A simple hand operated mounting carrying a single Oerlikon KAA 200 automatic cannon firing 1000 rounds/min. maximum range is 2000 m. Carried by most of the fleet's major warships except the Type 23 frigates.

20mm Mk.7A

The design of this simple but reliable weapon dates back to World War II but it still provides a useful increase in firepower, particularly for auxiliary vessels and RFAs. Rate of fire 500-800 rounds/min.

Torpedoes

Stingray

A lightweight anti submarine torpedo which can be launched from ships, helicopters or aircraft. In effect it is an undersea guided missile with a range of 11 km at 45 knots or 7.5 km at 60 knots. Length 2.1 m, diameter 330 mm. Aboard Type 42s and Type 22s Stingray is fired from triple tubes forming part of the Ships Torpedo Weapon System (STWS) but the newer Type 23s have the Magazine Torpedo Launch System (MTLS) with internal launch tubes.

Mk24 Tigerfish

A wire guided heavyweight torpedo carried by all Royal Navy submarines. Mainly designed for the anti-submarine role but its 134 kg warhead is equally effective against surface vessels. Propulsion is by means of a powerful two speed electric motor giving a range of 29 km at 24 knots or 13 km at 35 knots. Diameter is the standard 533 mm, and overall length approximately 6.5 m.

Spearfish

A complex heavyweight torpedo now entering service after a protracted and extensive development period. Claimed by the manufacturers to be the world's fastest torpedo, capable of over 70 kts, its sophisticated guidance system includes an onboard acoustic processing suite and tactical computer backed up by a command and control wire link to the parent submarine. Spearfish is fired from the standard submarine torpedo tube, but it is slightly shorter than Tigerfish and utilises an advanced turbine engine for higher performance.

At the end of the line ...

Readers may well find other warships afloat which are not mentioned in this book. The majority have fulfiled a long and useful life and are now relegated to non-seagoing duties. The following list gives details of their current duties:

Pennant No	Ship	Remarks
	BRITANNIA	Ex Royal Yacht at Leith. Open to the public.
A134	RAME HEAD	Escort Maintenance Vessel – Royal Marines Training Ship in Fareham Creek (Portsmouth)
C35	BELFAST	World War II Cruiser Museum ship – Pool of London Open to the public daily Tel: 0171-407 6434
D23	BRISTOL	Type 82 Destroyer – Sea Cadet Training Ship at Portsmouth.
D73	CAVALIER	World War II Destroyer Museum Ship at Hebburn Awaiting refurbishment and opening to the public at Chatham
F126	PLYMOUTH	Type 12 Frigate & Oberon class Submarine Museum Ships at Birkenhead, Wirral.
S21	ONYX	Open to the public daily. Tel: 0151 650 1573
M1115	BRONINGTON	Ton Class Minesweeper at Manchester Limited Opening to the Public Tel 0161 877 7778
S67	ALLIANCE	Submarine – Museum Ship at Gosport Open to the public daily. Tel: 01705 511485
M1151	IVESTON	(Thurrock) } Static Sea Cadet
M1154	KELLINGTON	(Stockton upon Tees) } Training Vessels

At the time of publishing (December 1998) the following ships were awaiting tow for scrap or sale.

PORTSMOUTH
Scylla
Wilton

PLYMOUTH
Conqueror
Courageous
Warspite
Valiant

ROSYTH
Churchill
Dreadnought
Revenge
Swiftsure
Resolution
Renown
Repulse

96